PETER PEPPER'S PET SPECTACULAR

written by Betty Paraskevas
paintings by Michael Paraskevas

All of the kids in the town loved to go
To Peter Pepper's Spectacular Show.
Now you must decide which pet will win,
So turn the page; we're about to begin.

MARIANNE PLATT AND HER CALICO CAT

Marianne Platt has a calico cat
Who wears blue satin trousers and plumes on his hat.
Maurice is his name
And he loves to sing
As he stands center stage
On his ball of string.

TOBY MCGRAW AND HERMAN THE MACAW

Toby McGraw
Has a pet macaw
Who speaks both Spanish and German.
He plays a guitar,
And shouts, "Wunderbar!"
As the crowd cries,
"Viva Herman!"

MELODY BARLOW AND HER WOOLLY PINK PIGLET

A woolly pink piglet
With a small velvet snout
Wears a lacy white bonnet,
With his ears sticking out.
There on the stage
He goes into his act.
That woolly pink piglet
Can add and subtract!

MICKEY DEANS AND FREDDIE THE BUNNY

Freddie is a bunny
Dressed like a clown.
When he tips his hat,
His pants fall down.

Jonathan Drake and Blake the Snake

When Blake the snake hears the music play,
He rises from his basket and begins to sway.
He wiggles to the left. He wiggles to the right.
He bows to the crowd when it's time to say, "Good night."

PENELOPE HICKS AND RICKY THE MUTT

Penelope Hicks taught Ricky some tricks,
He likes chasing the mailman instead.
He can sit up and beg,
And limp on one leg,
But the thing he does best is play dead.

Pamela Pickens and her Chickens

Pamela Pickens
Has three white chickens.
She dresses them in red, green, and blue.
One chicken flaps,
One chicken taps,
And one chicken plays the kazoo.

RANDY O'KEEFE AND HIS IRISH SETTER

An Irish setter in a turtleneck sweater
Has a talent the folks all enjoy.
Let the music begin,
Because he hopes to win
With a chorus of "Danny Boy."

Sue Ellen Rice and Her Three Tiny Mice

Sue Ellen Rice has three tiny mice,
Dressed up in cowboy suits.
They shout, "Yippee-ki-yay!"
Then, they hurry away,
Leaving only their tiny boots.

Priscilla Bruno and Louise the Pekingese

Louise, Louise,
A dainty Pekingese,
Flies through the air
With the greatest of ease.
She does it with style
And a Mona Lisa smile.
She's the star of the flying trapeze.

FONDA SNYDER AND CLARA THE SPIDER

Fonda Snyder has a fuzzy spider.
Clara bows when the spotlight goes on.
She moves to the blues,
In eight dancing shoes,
And the crowd breathes a sigh when she's gone.

Dawn Morningstar and Beauregard the St. Bernard

Beauregard the St. Bernard
Asks someone to pick a card.
Guessing the card brings Beauregard fame,
But all of the cards in his deck are the same.

The talent show's over.
It's time to begin
Choosing the pet
That you think should win.

for Priscilla Bruno,
a lovely lady

Published by Rainbow Bridge Publishing, P.O. Box 35665, Greensboro, NC 27425-5665

Printed in China.

The text for this book is set in Badger Medium.
The paintings are acrylic paint on rag paper.
The display type was hand-lettered by the illustrator.
Production supervision by Jennifer Weaver-Spencer.
Designed by Chasity Rice.

Library of Congress Cataloging-in-Publication Data

Paraskevas, Betty.
  Peter Pepper's pet spectacular / by Betty Paraskevas ; paintings by Michael Paraskevas.
     p. cm.
  Summary: Performing pets in colorful attire compete for the top prize in Peter Pepper's talent show.
  ISBN 978-1-60095-257-9
  [1. Pets--Fiction. 2. Animals--Fiction. 3. Talent shows--Fiction. 4. Stories in rhyme.] 1. Paraskevas, Michael, ill. 11. Title.
  PZ8.3.P162Pe 2007
  [E]--dc22
                  2007001045